Our State

Rise & Shine

BREAKFAST
in NORTH CAROLINA

EDITOR IN CHIEF: Elizabeth Hudson
OUR STATE RISE & SHINE LEAD EDITOR: Katie Schanze
EDITORS: Todd Dulaney, Lauren Eberle, Katie Kane, Mark Kemp,
Katie King, Chloe Klingstedt, Katie Saintsing
DESIGN DIRECTOR: Claudia Royston
ART DIRECTOR: Jason Chenier
ASSISTANT ART DIRECTOR: Hannah Wright
EDITORIAL DESIGNER: Erin LaBree
ART ASSISTANT: Claire Audilet

Our State

Rise & Shine

BREAKFAST
in NORTH CAROLINA

BELCROSS
BISCUIT
COMPANY
Camden

Consider this your wake-up call: In the Old North State, breakfast easily earns the distinction of being the most important — and delicious — meal of the day. Good morning, indeed.

22 *Breakfast* PLACES

Whether you prefer old-fashioned favorites or farm-to-table fare, a seat at one of these spots across the state is worthy of an early start.

HOMEGROWN
Asheville
Stand at the wall-size chalkboard and make your selection: The open-faced fried chicken biscuit covered in sausage gravy is unforgettable. Then, get comfy at a table in the wood-paneled dining room and have another mug of Black Mountain-roasted coffee.

371 Merrimon Avenue, (828) 232-4340

JOEY'S PANCAKE HOUSE
MAGGIE VALLEY

The signature pancakes — from classic blueberry to Reese's Cup to sweet potato — are still the star of the show at this beloved diner, which opened in 1966.

4309 Soco Road, (828) 926-0212

DAN'L BOONE INN
Boone

A Boone — and North Carolina — institution since 1959, the food here is served family-style, with heaping bowls of grits, country ham, bacon, sausage, scrambled eggs, buttermilk biscuits, and sausage or redeye gravy. The real treats, though, are the old-fashioned, freshly stewed apples, glazed cinnamon biscuits, and black cherry preserves. You can even buy a jar to take home.

130 Hardin Street, (828) 264-8657

PETER'S PANCAKES & WAFFLES
Cherokee

We love the classic laminated place mat menus that let you browse local businesses while you eat, and we also love the classic breakfast choices: short stacks with sausage links, eggs over easy, biscuits and gravy, and even corned-beef hash.

1384 Tsali Boulevard
(828) 497-5116

EARLY GIRL EATERY
Asheville

Early Girl Eatery partners with more than two dozen local farmers to provide home-style fare full of Asheville flavor, from abundant vegetarian and vegan selections to meat-lover favorites like the Porky Breakfast Bowl, made with barbecue, scrambled eggs, and local cheese.

8 Wall Street
(828) 259-9292 ext. 1

444 Haywood Road #101
(828) 259-9292 ext. 2

1378 Hendersonville Road, Suite A
(828) 259-9292 ext. 3

Windy City Grill
HICKORY

Homer Eckard owned this grill after World War II, and although he's gone and generations have passed, most people in Hickory still just call it Homer's. Today, the 75-year-old institution attracts a parade of regulars and students from nearby Lenoir-Rhyne University, who come each morning for, among other things, delicious breakfast sandwiches — like the sausage, egg, and double-cheese on a bun (above).

2514 North Center Street
(828) 322-1131

Who needs marshmallow pies? At Lucy in the Rye, dig into buttermilk-fried chicken on a Belgian waffle drizzled with hot honey.

LUCY IN THE RYE

Sylva

Try a chocolate waffle or a corned beef and cheddar omelet as you admire hundreds of colorful drawings. Instead of a children's menu, staff members give kids crayons and blank paper with the promise that whatever they draw will be proudly displayed.

612 West Main Street
(828) 586-4601

BISCUIT HEAD

Asheville

There will be a line at this Southern breakfast joint with a hipster twist. But no matter. Order the gravy "flight" — a sampler of three — or load up your biscuit at the jam-and-butter bar. The locally sourced food is worth the wait.

417 Biltmore Avenue, Suite 4F
(828) 505-3449

733 Haywood Road
(828) 333 5145

1994 Hendersonville Road
(828) 585-2055

Victory Kitchen

LAKE LURE

Rise and shine to country-style breakfast staples like bacon, eggs, grits, and pancakes — served with a smile and a prayer — at this Rutherford County restaurant that's known as much for its warm hospitality as its home-cooked Southern meals.

959 Buffalo Creek Road
(828) 436-5023

VICTORY KITCHEN
&
RESTAURANT

11

Krankies

Winston-Salem

Hope you're hungry: The Krankies Classic (pictured) — a biscuit stuffed with fried chicken (brined first in pickle juice, buttermilk, and Texas Pete) and drenched with Texas Pete and honey — is a one-handed meal.

211 East Third Street, (336) 722-3016

OLD RICHMOND GRILL
Pfafftown

Old Richmond first opened in 1955 as a drive-in. Since then, it hasn't changed much. Sit at the counter long enough, and it'll remind you of someone's front porch — if that front porch had cooked-to-order eggs and homemade gravy.

6425 Reynolda Road
(336) 924-4295

ELMO'S DINER
Durham

Elmo's serves from-scratch comfort dishes the way you love them — and in big portions. Get there early and grab a booth to watch the morning unfold. Or get there late and sip a hot cup of coffee while you wait.

776 9th Street
(919) 416-3823

FRANKLINVILLE DINER
Franklinville

A sweet way to start the day: grilled vanilla pound cake. At this family-owned restaurant, each thick wedge is prepared to order, grilled in butter on the flat-top until a crispy golden crust forms.

159 West Main Street
(336) 824-2117

SUNRISE BISCUIT KITCHEN
CHAPEL HILL

The queue of cars awaiting a turn at the drive-through window can cause a traffic jam, especially on Tar Heel game days and alumni weekends. Fans note that the ratio of chicken to biscuit is pretty even, ensuring a bit of both in every bite. The biscuit, hash brown, and sweet tea combo is a popular order. But don't forget a cinnamon roll made with biscuit dough to snack on later.

1305 East Franklin Street
(919) 933-1324

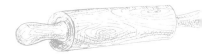

Old Bridge Diner

OAK ISLAND

You rent a beach house for the week, and you know the drill: Stop by the local grocery for a few perishables — beer's a perishable, right? — figure out the closest fish market for fresh shrimp, and get ready for a week of simple meals.

If your rental is in the town of Oak Island or next-door Caswell Beach, though, you need to add a stop: the Old Bridge Diner, right next to the G.V. Barbee Bridge.

The Old Bridge is the spot for beach-morning breakfasts and lunches, a classic diner with a

Order a Loaded Biscuit (opposite) at the Old Bridge Diner before crossing over the G.V. Barbee Bridge.

faux-tin ceiling, a quilted chrome backsplash, and a long counter. It's the kind of place where regulars take over a corner booth to hash out the world's problems over hash browns and eggs or drop in to pick up a burger to go for lunch. Or to grab a gallon — yes, really — of clam chowder to take back to their beach house.

The time doesn't matter, actually: Owner Michael Jones designed the menu to cover both breakfast and lunch from 6 a.m. to 2 p.m. daily. "You can get a cheeseburger at 6 a.m. or an omelet at 1:30 in the afternoon," he says.

In addition to the classic clam chowder, which is so good that you could probably eat it cold, the menu is filled with Benedicts, pancakes, waffles, sandwiches, and fried seafood. The popular Loaded Biscuit is an open-faced biscuit topped with two sausage patties, hash browns, Cheddar cheese, sausage gravy, and

eggs. (You can get a half version, too, if you're not planning to nap right after breakfast.)

— *Kathleen Purvis*

132 Country Club Drive
(910) 250-1184

The Country Biscuit

NEW BERN

The whole menu is delicious, but don't skip the biscuit doughnut holes: biscuit dough deep-fried to a golden brown and covered with a sugary glaze (and sometimes coconut shavings).

809 Broad Street, (252) 638-5151

SAM & OMIE'S
Nags Head

Capt. Sambo Tillet opened Sambo's to serve breakfast to other local fishermen. He later added the name of his son, also a fisherman. Today, customers still come in for their morning "Omie-lettes."

7228 South Virginia Dare Trail
(252) 441-7366

MOM'S GRILL
Washington

The buttery yellow exterior of Mom's Grill in Washington is an apt advertisement for the golden biscuits baked inside.

True to eastern North Carolina tradition, each comes stuffed with a thick wedge of melted sharp Cheddar.

1041 John Small Avenue
(252) 946-2260

BELCROSS BISCUIT COMPANY
Camden

Try local favorite The Jess: egg, cheese, sausage, grape jelly, and mustard on a perfectly golden, regionally famous sweet potato biscuit.

269 U.S. Highway 158 East
(252) 338-1286

FLO'S KITCHEN

Wilson

Flo's serves cathead biscuits, so named because they are the size of a cat's head. Good homemade biscuits require a lot of hand-holding, and those at Flo's are no exception. It takes two hands to make them, and two hands to eat them.

1015 Goldsboro Street South, (252) 237-9146

Baker's Kitchen

NEW BERN

Chicken and waffles
(opposite) make
a perfect vehicle
for Butter Syrup at
Baker's Kitchen, where
breakfast is king.

Dip. Dunk. Drizzle. Over and onto fried chicken, sausage, and, of course, pancakes, waffles, French toast, and anything with a bready texture, the better to absorb the sugary, buttery, palomino-pony-colored "craft syrup" that is Baker's Kitchen's signature condiment: Butter Syrup. "Move over, maple!" reads the label. While the recipe is what the owners politely call "proprietary," here's a secret: There's not a drop of maple syrup in the potion. And if your sweet tooth still isn't satisfied? There's always the homemade grilled cinnamon roll covered in icing.

— *Susan Stafford Kelly*

227 Middle Street
(252) 637-0304

19

The Pig

RICHLANDS

ollard Man pipes right up. "Look here," he says, leaning over a country diner table, fixing me with a serious gaze. "We talk about important stuff every day. Like: How do they get the different-colored stripes of toothpaste inside the toothpaste tube? Do you know? Have you ever asked yourself that question?"

Appreciative murmurs rumble around a pair of red-and-white tables jumbled with coffee cups, plates of eggs, munched-on biscuits, and crunched-on bacon. Seven or eight men crowd around, like an eastern North Carolina version of The Last Supper. There's a lot of head-nodding. A fair number of sheepish grins.

"Mysteries of the world," intones another fellow. "That's what we struggle with here."

These fellows do their best to stifle grins, but the laughter comes quickly, hoots and

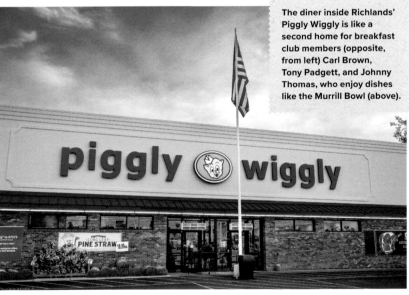

The diner inside Richlands' Piggly Wiggly is like a second home for breakfast club members (opposite, from left) Carl Brown, Tony Padgett, and Johnny Thomas, who enjoy dishes like the Murrill Bowl (above).

hollers that jostle coffee and turn over at least one packet of strawberry jelly.

Collard Man's real name is Wayne Barbee, I learn. He's known for his status as a long-time member of one of the most prestigious, sought-after — heck, even elite — social and cultural clubs in the region: The early morning, two-table gathering of regulars at the Piggly Wiggly diner in downtown Richlands.

"The Pig," it's called, and every day but Sunday, breakfast starts promptly at 5:30 a.m. This group gathers every morning in two shifts — early and late.

Let me tell you what's on the breakfast menu at The Pig. There's country ham, bacon piled up like timber on a logging deck, two kinds of link sausage (smoked and fresh), scrambled eggs with cheese, scrambled eggs without cheese, plain grits, cheese grits, potato wedges, biscuits and gravy, and cooked apples. There's more, but I'm too hungry to pay closer attention. I've been advised to forgo the plate breakfast and put in an order for a Murrill Bowl — a large cup of grits, cheese, and eggs, with a choice of bacon or fresh sausage. It's named for one of the ancestors of Richlands' Sylvester family, owners of the Piggly Wiggly and caretakers of its 65-year-old mystique. Who in their right mind would turn down a Murrill Bowl?

The food is very good, but there's a different sort of sustenance being served up at The Pig, and it's no less palpable than the scent of sausage on a hot flat-top. Every morning, there's a sort of communion set on those red-topped tables. It feeds the soul as much as the body. — *T. Edward Nickens*

8406 Richlands Highway
(910) 324-3333

OAK HILL ON
LOVE LANE
Waynesville

5
Incredible
B&B
Breakfasts

Where you lay your head at night is only
half of the bed and breakfast experience.
At these five inns, the recipe for a great stay
includes an elaborate morning spread.

written by REBECCA WOLTZ

At Oak Hill on Love Lane, Ann Kitzis takes care of people with breakfast served on her wraparound porch overlooking a photo-worthy view of the Smokies.

Oak Hill on Love Lane

WAYNESVILLE

Anna Kitzis didn't know what grits were until she moved to western North Carolina from Boston. But after settling in Waynesville and buying Oak Hill on Love Lane in 2019, she realized that she'd been eating the Southern favorite all her life, though she'd called it by a different name. Her father, who was from Ukraine, had taught her how to make a cornmeal porridge called *mamaliga*. When he wanted cheesy mamaliga, he would add feta — not so different from cheesy grits.

Kitzis often asks guests if they'd like to try eating something outside of their comfort zone, like Eastern European-style stuffed crepes, a nod to Kitzis's Polish and Russian roots. She stuffs the crepes with farmers cheese and raisins and sweetens them with monk fruit or maple syrup. For those who aren't the experimenting type, though, she's just as happy to whip up some grits.

224 Love Lane
(824) 456-7037

HANNA HOUSE BED & BREAKFAST
New Bern
The first course at breakfast is fruit, like pears purchased at the New Bern Farmers Market and poached with butter and honey from owner Camille Klotz's own beehives, then topped with pistachios. Main courses rotate, with more than a dozen offered at any given time. If you're lucky, one of those just might be Klotz's savory French toast.
218 Pollock Street
(252) 635-3209

FOLKESTONE INN
Bryson City
The inn's huevos rancheros (below) feature house-made sausage, pico de gallo with garden-grown tomatoes, and eggs from the inn's own chickens.
101 Folkestone Road
(828) 488-2730

THE IVY
Warrenton
The coffee table in The Ivy's front parlor is set with china. A teapot sits snug in its Union Jack-decorated tea cozy. Owner Karen Kelley delivers the second of three courses for an English tea: a three-tiered stand stacked with lemon meringue cookies, miniature tarts, and warm scones ready to be smeared with clotted cream and jam.
331 North Main Street
(252) 257-9300

1898 WAVERLY INN
Hendersonville
The scent of warm vanilla fills the kitchen of the inn as a double waffle iron bakes blueberry buttermilk batter into waffles, extra crispy on the outside and moist and fluffy on the inside. They're dusted with a layer of powdered sugar before being served to guests.
783 North Main Street
(828) 693-9193

31 Breakfast RECIPES

From simple sweet potato biscuits to decadent baked French toast with a crunchy blueberry topping, you're sure to wake up on the right side of the bed when you start your day with one of these delicious breakfast dishes.

original recipes by LYNN WELLS
photography by MATT HULSMAN

**SWEET POTATO HASH
WITH SAUSAGE & EGGS**
PAGE 79

Baked French Toast Casserole

Yield: 10 servings.

- 1 (12- to 14-ounce) loaf French, sourdough, or challah bread, cut into 1-inch cubes
- 8 ounces cream cheese, room temperature
- 2 tablespoons powdered sugar
- 2 teaspoons vanilla extract, divided
- 8 large eggs
- 2¼ cups whole milk
- ½ teaspoon ground cinnamon
- ½ teaspoon ground nutmeg
- ⅔ cup packed dark brown sugar
- 1 teaspoon orange extract

TOPPING:
- ⅓ cup packed dark brown sugar
- ⅓ cup all-purpose flour
- ½ teaspoon ground cinnamon
- 6 tablespoons cold unsalted butter, cut into small cubes

GARNISH:
- Fresh orange slices
- Powdered sugar

Grease a 9 x 13-inch dish with butter or nonstick spray. Spread half of the cubes into the prepared dish.

Using an electric mixer, beat cream cheese on medium-high speed until completely smooth. Beat in the powdered sugar and ¼ teaspoon vanilla extract until combined. Drop spoonfuls of cream cheese mixture evenly on top of the bread. Layer the remaining bread cubes on top of cream cheese. Set aside.

Whisk together the eggs, milk, cinnamon, nutmeg, brown sugar, remaining vanilla, and orange extract until mixture is smooth. Pour mixture over the bread. Cover the pan tightly with plastic wrap and refrigerate for at least 3 hours and up to overnight.

Preheat oven to 350°. Remove dish from the refrigerator.

For the topping: In a medium bowl, whisk together the brown sugar, flour, and cinnamon. Cut in the cold cubed butter with a pastry blender or two forks. Sprinkle the topping over the soaked bread.

Bake, uncovered, for 45 to 55 minutes or until golden brown on top. Serve immediately with fresh orange slices and a dusting of powdered sugar.

Pecan Crunch Coffee Cake

Yield: 10 to 12 servings.

TOPPING:
- ½ cup pecans, chopped
- 1 teaspoon ground cinnamon
- ½ cup sugar

BATTER:
- 2 sticks unsalted butter, softened
- ½ cup sugar
- 6 large eggs
- 2 teaspoons vanilla extract
- 5 cups all-purpose flour
- 4½ teaspoons baking powder
- 1 teaspoon salt
- 1 pint heavy cream

FILLING:
- 2 cups powdered sugar, sifted
- 1½ cups pecans, chopped
- 2 teaspoons ground cinnamon

Preheat oven to 350°. Grease and flour 2 loaf pans. Tap pans to remove excess flour.

For the topping: Mix all ingredients and set aside.

For the batter: Combine butter and ½ cup sugar in a large mixing bowl. Mix on high until creamy, about 3 minutes.

Add eggs, one at a time, mixing well after each addition. Add vanilla and mix.

In a separate bowl, sift together flour, baking powder and salt. Alternate adding dry ingredients and cream to batter, beginning and ending with dry ingredients.

For the filling: Combine ingredients in separate bowl.

Sprinkle half of the filling on bottom and sides of pans. Pour half the batter over filling. Sprinkle remaining filling over batter. Pour in remaining batter. Top each pan with topping mixture. Bake at 350° for 1 hour and 15 minutes or until knife inserted in cake comes out clean. Let stand 15 minutes before removing from pans, then place loaves on rack to cool.

Honey Buns

Yield: 15 buns.

DOUGH:

- 1 **(2¼-teaspoon) packet yeast**
- 1⅓ **cups water (112° to 115°)**
- ⅓ **cup honey**
- 4 **teaspoons unsalted butter**
- ⅓ **teaspoon cinnamon**
- ⅓ **teaspoon ground ginger**
- 1 **teaspoon salt**
- 4 **cups all-purpose flour**

In a medium bowl, add yeast to water and stir. Allow to sit for 5 minutes, or until a foam forms on top.

Place all ingredients in the mixing bowl of an electric mixer. Using a dough hook, mix ingredients until the dough forms a ball, pulling away from the sides of the mixing bowl.

Pour dough onto a clean countertop and divide (or cut) into 15 pieces. To keep dough portions from drying out, cover with a clean dish towel or plastic wrap. Working with one piece at a time, roll dough into snakes and coil them, moistening the "tail" and pressing it down on the edge to make a coiled bun. Keep the other pieces covered until all are coiled.

Place dough on baking sheets lined with parchment paper. Place in a warm, draft-free place until they have doubled in size. (Tip: Turn the oven light on and set a pan of hot water on the lower rack. Place baking sheets with dough on top shelf of oven to rise.)

Remove pans from oven. Preheat oven to 400°. Bake for about 15 minutes, or until lightly browned.

GLAZE:

- 2 **cups powdered sugar**
- 1 **teaspoon vanilla extract**
- 1 **tablespoon honey**
- 3 **tablespoons whole milk (may use more or less for desired consistency)**

Mix all ingredients and drizzle on buns after cooling. Glaze should firm to the consistency of doughnut icing.

Pumpkin Pie Pancakes

Yield: 8 pancakes.

- 1½ cups milk
- 1 cup canned pumpkin
- 1 egg
- 2 tablespoons salted butter, melted
- 2 tablespoons white vinegar
- 2 cups all-purpose flour
- 3 tablespoons brown sugar
- 2 teaspoons baking powder
- 1 teaspoon baking soda
- 1 teaspoon ground allspice
- 1½ teaspoons ground cinnamon
- 1 teaspoon ground ginger
- ½ teaspoon salt
- Whipped cream (for garnish)
- Toasted walnuts (for garnish)
- Maple Syrup (for garnish)

In a bowl, mix milk, pumpkin, egg, butter, and vinegar.

In a separate bowl, combine flour, brown sugar, baking powder, baking soda, allspice, cinnamon, ginger, and salt. Stir into the pumpkin mixture just enough to combine. Do not overmix.

Heat a lightly oiled griddle or frying pan over medium-high heat. Pour or scoop the batter onto the griddle, using approximately ¼ cup for each pancake. Brown on both sides and serve hot. Top with whipped cream, toasted walnuts, and maple syrup, if desired.

Sweet Potato Muffins

Yield: 12 muffins.

- **1¼ cups packed light brown sugar**
- **½ cup canola oil**
- **1 teaspoon vanilla extract**
- **2 eggs**
- **2 cups all-purpose flour**
- **2 teaspoons baking powder**
- **1 teaspoon ground cinnamon**
- **1 teaspoon freshly grated nutmeg**
- **½ teaspoon ground allspice**
- **1 teaspoon salt**
- **2 (15-ounce) cans sweet potato, drained**
- **½ cup raisins (optional)**
- **1 cup walnuts (optional)**

Preheat oven to 350°. Grease muffin tins to hold 12 muffins.

In a small bowl, whisk together brown sugar, oil, vanilla, and eggs. Set aside.

Mix together the flour, baking powder, cinnamon, nutmeg, allspice, salt, and sweet potatoes in a large bowl. Make a well in the center, and pour in the egg mixture. Stir the egg mixture, gradually incorporating it with the flour mixture. If desired, stir in the raisins and walnuts.

Spoon the batter into the tins and fill to the top. Bake the muffins for 25 to 30 minutes or until a toothpick inserted into the middle comes out clean. Remove the muffins from the oven and run a paring knife carefully around each muffin. Invert the pan to release the muffins. Serve immediately.

Glazed Cranberry-Orange Scones

Yield: 12 scones.

¾   **pound cold salted butter, cut into small cubes**

4¼   **cups all-purpose flour, divided**

½   **cup sugar**

2   **tablespoons baking powder**

1   **teaspoon kosher salt**

2   **tablespoons grated orange zest**

5   **large eggs, lightly beaten**

1   **cup cold heavy cream**

1   **cup fresh cranberries, rinsed**

1   **egg beaten with 2 tablespoons water, for egg wash**

½   **cup coarse or sparkling sugar**

½   **cup powdered sugar, plus 2 tablespoons**

4   **teaspoons freshly squeezed orange juice**

Preheat oven to 425°. Place cubed butter in freezer for 10 to 15 minutes.

In the bowl of an electric mixer, whisk together 4 cups of flour, ½ cup sugar, baking powder, salt, and orange zest. Using the paddle attachment, add cold butter and mix at low speed until the mixture resembles coarse cornmeal.

In a small bowl, whisk together the eggs and heavy cream. Gradually add the egg mixture to the flour and butter mixture. Mix on low speed until just blended; do not overmix.

Pat the cranberries dry with a paper towel. In a medium bowl, toss the cranberries with ¼ cup of flour. Fold cranberries into dough.

Place the dough onto a floured surface and knead it into a ball. Flour your hands and a rolling pin and roll the dough to a 2-inch-thick square. Fold the dough over, lightly roll it, and fold it over again. Roll the dough to 1-inch thickness. Flour a 3-inch round cutter and cut circles of dough. Place the scones on a parchment-lined baking pan. Use scraps to form a ball, roll it out, and cut until all dough has been used.

Brush the tops of the scones with egg wash, sprinkle with coarse sugar, and bake for 20 minutes. The tops should be golden brown and the insides fully baked. Allow scones to cool for 30 minutes. Whisk together powdered sugar and orange juice, and drizzle over the scones.

Pumpkin Biscuits
With Orange-Honey Butter

Yield: 12 biscuits.

- **2 cups all-purpose flour**
- **3 tablespoons sugar**
- **2 teaspoons baking powder**
- **1 teaspoon ground cinnamon**
- **½ teaspoon baking soda**
- **½ teaspoon salt**
- **¼ teaspoon ground nutmeg**
- **¼ cup cold salted butter, cut into small pieces**
- **¾ cup whole milk**
- **½ cup canned pumpkin**

Preheat oven to 450°. Combine flour, baking powder, cinnamon, baking soda, salt, and nutmeg; cut in butter with a pastry blender or two knives until mixture resembles coarse sand.

Combine milk and pumpkin, and add to flour mixture, stirring until just moist. Turn out the dough onto a heavily floured surface. Knead lightly five times. Flour a rolling pin and roll dough to about ½-inch thickness. Cut into 12 biscuits with a 2½-inch biscuit cutter.

Place the biscuits on a parchment-lined baking sheet. Bake at 450° for 11 minutes, or until golden.

ORANGE-HONEY BUTTER

Yield: 1 cup.

- **½ cup salted butter, softened**
- **½ cup honey**
- **½ teaspoon orange zest**
- **⅛ teaspoon salt**

Combine all ingredients and mix well. Butter may be served at room temperature or chilled. Great on biscuits, pancakes, vegetables, chicken, and fish.

Baked French Toast
With Blueberry Crunch

Yield: 6 servings.

- **2 tablespoons butter, softened**
- **6 eggs**
- **2 cups half-and-half**
- **2 teaspoons cinnamon**
- **¼ teaspoon freshly ground nutmeg**
- **1 teaspoon vanilla extract**
- **½ teaspoon salt**
- **1 large loaf French bread, cut into 2-inch cubes (day-old preferred)**
- **1 (8-ounce) package cream cheese, cut into cubes**

BLUEBERRY TOPPING:

- **2 cups fresh or frozen blueberries**
- **½ cup maple syrup**
- **½ cup sugar**
- **4 tablespoons cornstarch**
- **1½ cups crushed corn flakes**
- **¼ cup powdered sugar (for garnish)**

Lightly spread butter in a 9 x 13-inch casserole dish, making sure to get all four corners of the pan.

In a large bowl, whisk together eggs, half-and-half, cinnamon, nutmeg, vanilla, and salt.

Place half of the bread cubes in prepared dish. Top with half of the cream cheese cubes. Add remaining bread cubes and top with remaining cream cheese. Pour egg mixture over bread cubes, pressing down so that the bread is completely soaked by the egg mixture.

Cover with plastic wrap and chill in refrigerator for 3 hours or overnight.

Preheat oven to 375°. In a medium bowl, add blueberries and maple syrup. Sprinkle sugar and cornstarch over blueberries and toss so they are evenly coated. Spread blueberries evenly over bread mixture. Cover casserole with foil and bake for 30 minutes.

Remove foil; sprinkle corn flakes over the top. Bake an additional 20 to 30 minutes or until center is firm and cereal is crispy.

Let cool slightly and sprinkle with powdered sugar. Serve with maple or blueberry syrup.

Ginger Spice Scones

Yield: 6 scones.

- **2** cups all-purpose flour
- **2** teaspoons baking powder
- **½** teaspoon baking soda
- **½** teaspoon salt
- **1** teaspoon ground cinnamon
- **½** teaspoon ground coriander
- **1** teaspoon ground cardamom
- **¼** teaspoon ground cloves
- **4** tablespoons unsalted butter, very cold, cut into small pieces
- **½** cup crystallized ginger, chopped into pea-size pieces
- **¾** cup heavy cream
- **¼** cup packed dark brown sugar
- **1** large egg, beaten, for egg wash
- Coarse or sparkling sugar (optional)

Preheat oven to 425°. Line a baking sheet with parchment paper.

In a medium bowl, whisk together the flour, baking powder, baking soda, salt, and spices. Add the cold butter, tossing to coat with the dry ingredients. With your fingers, press the butter pieces into the flour mixture until all of the butter is incorporated. The butter pieces should resemble small leaves. Add the ginger and gently toss to combine.

In a small bowl, whisk together the cream and brown sugar. Add the wet mixture to the dry ingredients and mix gently with your hands until just combined. The dough should be firm and barely cohesive.

Transfer the dough to a lightly floured work surface and fold a few times to incorporate any dry bits, if necessary. Pat the dough into a circle 1 inch thick and 7 inches across. Wrap the dough in clear plastic wrap and refrigerate for 10 to 15 minutes.

Remove dough from refrigerator and cut into 6 wedges, using a chef's knife to cut directly down. Arrange the scones evenly on the prepared baking sheet. Brush the top of each scone with egg wash and top with coarse sugar, if desired.

Bake scones for 18 to 22 minutes on the top rack, rotating the baking sheet after 14 minutes, until they're light gold and slightly firm to the touch. Remove scones from oven and serve warm or at room temperature.

Maple-Pecan Coffee Cake

Yield: 6 servings.

CRUMBLE:

- ½ cup dark brown sugar
- ¼ cup all-purpose flour
- ¼ cup pecans, chopped
- ½ teaspoon ground cinnamon
- ½ teaspoon salt
- 3 tablespoons unsalted butter, melted

COFFEE CAKE:

- 2 cups all-purpose flour
- 1 teaspoon baking powder
- ½ teaspoon baking soda
- ½ teaspoon salt
- ½ cup light brown sugar
- ½ cup pecans, chopped
- ½ cup pure maple syrup
- ½ cup vegetable oil
- ¼ cup whole milk
- 2 large eggs, beaten
- 1 teaspoon maple extract (can be found at specialty kitchen stores)
- ½ teaspoon vanilla extract
- 8 ounces sour cream, at room temperature

ICING:

- 1 cup powdered sugar
- 2 tablespoons maple syrup

For the crumble: In a small bowl, combine brown sugar, flour, pecans, cinnamon, and salt. Mix well using a fork. Use fork to stir while you pour in melted butter until a crumb-like texture forms. Break up any large crumbs with fork.

For the coffee cake: Preheat oven to 350°. Prepare an 8-inch square pan with nonstick cooking spray. In a large bowl, stir together flour, baking powder, baking soda, salt, brown sugar, and pecans. In a small bowl, stir together the maple syrup, vegetable oil, milk, eggs, and extracts. Stir the sour cream into the wet ingredients until combined.

Make a well in the center of the dry ingredients, then pour in the wet ingredients. Gently stir until just combined. Do not overmix. Spoon half of the batter into the prepared pan. Sprinkle with half of the crumble. Spread the remaining batter over the crumble. Sprinkle with the remaining crumble.

Bake for 35 minutes or until a toothpick inserted in the center comes out clean. Cool for 15 minutes.

For the icing: In a small bowl, combine powdered sugar and maple syrup until a thick, pourable icing forms. Drizzle icing over warm cake. Cut into squares and serve. Store leftovers, covered, at room temperature for up to 4 days.

Brown Sugar Breakfast Tarts

Yield: 6 tarts.

DOUGH:
- 2½ cups all-purpose flour
- 1 teaspoon salt
- 1 teaspoon granulated sugar
- ¾ cup unsalted butter, chilled and cubed
- 6 tablespoons vegetable shortening, chilled
- 4 to 5 tablespoons ice water

FILLING:
- ½ cup light brown sugar
- 2 teaspoons ground cinnamon
- 1 tablespoon all-purpose flour
- 1 tablespoon unsalted butter, melted
- 2 teaspoons maple syrup

ICING:
- 1 cup powdered sugar
- 1 teaspoon ground cinnamon
- ¼ teaspoon vanilla extract
- 2 tablespoons whole milk

For the dough: In a large bowl, whisk together flour, salt, and sugar. Using two forks or a pastry cutter, cut butter and shortening into the flour mixture. After a few minutes, the flour will resemble a sand-like consistency with a few medium-size lumps.

Add in 2 tablespoons of ice water and combine using a rubber spatula. Gently mix in 2 more tablespoons of ice water. The dough should come together and form a mass, but still easily fall apart. It's ready when the dough starts to stick to the spatula.

Scrape dough out onto a lightly floured surface. Form into a rectangular shape and cut in half. Wrap each half separately in plastic wrap and refrigerate for at least 2 hours or overnight.

After dough has chilled, take one half out of the fridge and let it sit at room temperature for about 15 minutes. On a floured surface, roll dough out to about 9 x 13 inches and ⅛-inch thickness. Using a pizza cutter, slice six 3 x 4-inch rectangles and transfer to a small tray lined with parchment paper. Place in the fridge and repeat for the second half of dough for a total of 12 rectangles.

For the filling: In a small bowl, combine all of the ingredients and preheat oven to 350°.

Take 6 of the dough rectangles out of the fridge and place them, evenly spaced, on a large baking sheet lined with parchment paper. Add 1 tablespoon filling to the center of each rectangle. Spread it evenly, leaving about ½ an inch around the edges.

Take the remaining 6 rectangles out of the fridge and use a toothpick to poke 6 to 7 holes into each. Set aside.

Dab the edges of the filled rectangles with cold water and place the perforated rectangles on top. Gently press the edges to seal. Crimp the edges with a fork, then bake for 25 to 28 minutes. They should come out dull on top with a slightly golden edge. Cool tarts on the baking sheet for about 10 minutes, then transfer to a cooling rack.

For the icing: In a small bowl, combine all of the ingredients and mix until smooth. Spoon into the center of the cooled tarts and gently spread toward the edges. The icing will be thin enough to run down the sides. Sprinkle with a little cinnamon sugar, if desired.

Orange & Ginger Oatmeal With Toasted Walnuts

Yield: 4 servings.

- **1 tablespoon unsalted butter**
- **1 tablespoon brown sugar**
- **¼ cup walnuts, chopped**
- **1 cup milk (low-fat, whole, or almond milk)**
- **2½ cups water, plus more as needed**
- **1 cup steel-cut oats**
- **½ teaspoon kosher salt**
- **1 teaspoon fresh orange zest, plus more for garnish**
- **½ teaspoon ground ginger**
- **¼ teaspoon ground cinnamon**

In a small saucepan, melt butter on medium heat. Add brown sugar and stir until dissolved. Add chopped walnuts and stir until evenly coated in sugar mixture. Reduce heat and continue stirring walnuts until they begin to smell toasted. Remove from heat and set aside.

In a large saucepan, combine milk and 2½ cups water. Bring to a boil over high heat. Stir the oats and salt into the boiling water. Return mixture to a steady boil, then reduce heat to low or simmer.

Gently simmer for 20 minutes, stirring occasionally and scraping the bottom of the pan to prevent sticking. For softer, creamier oats, continue cooking for 5 to 10 additional minutes, stirring every few minutes. If the oatmeal becomes too thick, add water or milk to thin it out to desired consistency.

Remove oatmeal from heat and let sit a few minutes to thicken. Stir in orange zest, ginger, and cinnamon. Serve oatmeal with additional orange zest and the toasted walnuts. Store leftovers in refrigerator for up to 5 days.

Buttermilk & Apple Pancakes

Yield: 4 servings.

- **2 cups all-purpose flour**
- **1 teaspoon baking soda**
- **2 teaspoons baking powder**
- **3 tablespoons dark brown sugar**
- **1 teaspoon salt**
- **1 teaspoon ground cinnamon**
- **2 large eggs**
- **1½ cups buttermilk**
- **½ cup sour cream**
- **¼ cup unsalted butter, melted**
- **1 large Honeycrisp or Pink Lady apple, peeled, cored, and grated (about 2 cups)**

APPLE TOPPING:

- **1 large Honeycrisp or Pink Lady apple, peeled, cored, and thinly sliced**
- **2 teaspoons fresh lemon juice**
- **2 tablespoons unsalted butter**
- **Whipped topping (for garnish)**
- **Cinnamon (for dusting)**

For the pancakes: In a large bowl, mix together flour, baking soda, baking powder, brown sugar, salt, and cinnamon.

In another bowl, whisk together eggs, buttermilk, sour cream, and melted butter; add to flour mixture and stir until flour is just moistened. Stir in grated apple.

Drop ¼ cup of batter at a time onto a hot, lightly greased griddle. When bubbles start to appear in the batter, flip the pancake and cook for 1 minute. Repeat with remaining batter.

For the topping: Mix together apple slices and lemon juice.

In a skillet, melt butter, add the apple slices, and cook on medium heat until apples are just tender, about 2 to 3 minutes. Top pancakes with cooked apples, and finish with whipped topping and a sprinkle of cinnamon.

Hot Skillet Pancakes

Yield: 12 pancakes.

2 cups all-purpose flour
2 teaspoons baking powder
½ teaspoon baking soda
½ teaspoon salt
¼ cup granulated sugar
2 cups whole buttermilk
2 large eggs, at room temperature
3 tablespoons butter, melted, plus more for frying
Fresh fruit and maple syrup (optional)

In a large bowl, whisk together flour, baking powder, baking soda, salt, and sugar.

In a small bowl, whisk together buttermilk, eggs, and butter. Add to the flour mixture and stir until just combined. Don't overmix.

Heat a skillet (preferably cast iron) or griddle over medium-high heat. Add a generous pat of butter to the hot skillet. Drop ¼ cup of batter into the skillet, then reduce heat to medium. Cook until bubbles form across the top of the pancake, then flip and continue to cook until golden brown, about 2 to 3 minutes per side. Repeat with remaining batter.

Serve with fresh fruit and warm maple syrup, if desired.

Bacon & Cheddar Mini Muffins

Yield: 36 mini muffins.

- 2 cups all-purpose flour
- 2 teaspoons baking powder
- 1 teaspoon salt
- ½ teaspoon freshly ground black pepper
- ½ teaspoon onion powder
- 1¼ cups shredded extra-sharp Cheddar cheese, divided
- ¼ cup butter
- 1 cup whole buttermilk
- 1 large egg
- 6 strips bacon, cooked crispy, chopped
- 2 tablespoons fresh chives, chopped

Preheat oven to 400°. Grease a 24-cup and a 12-cup mini muffin pan. In a bowl, whisk together flour, baking powder, salt, pepper, and onion powder. Add 1 cup cheese and stir.

In a saucepan, melt butter on low heat; add buttermilk and simmer for 1 to 2 minutes. Remove from heat and let sit for 5 minutes.

While whisking buttermilk mixture, add egg and continue whisking until ingredients are well blended. Gradually add buttermilk mixture to flour mixture and stir. Add chopped bacon and mix until just combined.

Spoon batter into prepared muffin pans, filling cups to just below the tops. Sprinkle muffin tops with remaining ¼ cup cheese. Bake 12 to 15 minutes or until a toothpick comes out clean. Garnish with chopped chives. Serve hot or warm.

Spinach & Sausage Bread Pudding

Yield: 8 to 10 servings.

- **1 loaf brioche bread**
- **1 pound ground breakfast sausage, cooked and drained**
- **1 tablespoon unsalted butter**
- **2 cups onion, chopped**
- **3 cups fresh baby spinach**
- **2 cups Gruyère cheese, grated**
- **12 large eggs**
- **1½ cups half-and-half**
- **1 teaspoon Dijon mustard**
- **1 teaspoon salt**
- **½ teaspoon freshly ground black pepper**

Prepare a 9 x 13-inch casserole dish with cooking spray. Tear brioche into large chunks and place in dish, overlapping to cover the bottom. Sprinkle cooked sausage on top of bread and distribute evenly.

In a skillet, melt the butter on medium heat and add onions. Cook onions for about 5 minutes or until soft. Add spinach to pan and cook until spinach is just wilted. Pour cooked onions and spinach over top of sausage. Top with grated cheese.

In a bowl, whisk together the eggs and half-and-half. Add mustard, salt, and pepper. Pour the egg mixture over the bread in the pan. Cover with plastic wrap and refrigerate overnight.

The next morning, remove casserole from fridge, preheat oven to 375°, and place rack in middle position. Remove plastic wrap and cover baking dish with foil. Bake, covered, for 30 minutes. Remove foil and bake until top is slightly puffy and center is set, about 30 minutes more.

Let cool for about 10 minutes. Serve immediately.

Shrimp & Cheese Grits Casserole

Yield: 4 servings.

- **4** cups chicken broth
- **1½** teaspoons kosher salt, divided
- **1** cup yellow stone-ground grits
- **½** cup half-and-half
- **¼** cup cooking sherry
- **1** cup sharp cheese, shredded
- **1** cup Gouda, shredded
- **2** large eggs, lightly beaten
- **2** tablespoons olive oil, divided
- **2** tablespoons unsalted butter, divided
- **6** green onions, chopped
- **1** medium sweet onion, chopped
- **1** celery stalk, chopped
- **1** red bell pepper, chopped
- **1** clove garlic, minced
- **1** teaspoon ground black pepper, divided
- **1** pound medium fresh shrimp, peeled, tails left on
- **1** teaspoon smoked paprika
- **¼** teaspoon freshly grated nutmeg

Preheat oven to 350°. In a large saucepan, combine broth and ½ teaspoon salt. Bring mixture to a rolling boil; stir in grits. Cover, reduce heat to medium, and cook, stirring occasionally, until liquid is absorbed and grits are tender, about 20 minutes. Stir in half-and-half, sherry, and cheese; remove from heat. Gradually whisk in eggs until smooth.

In a 10-inch cast-iron skillet, heat 1 tablespoon olive oil and 1 tablespoon butter over medium-high heat. Add onions, celery, red bell pepper, garlic, ½ teaspoon salt, and ½ teaspoon black pepper. Cook, stirring frequently, until tender, about 5 minutes. Add grits mixture to onion mixture; stir to combine. Bake until set, approximately 30 to 35 minutes. Remove from oven and allow to sit for 10 minutes.

In a nonstick skillet, heat remaining olive oil over medium-high heat. Sprinkle shrimp with ½ teaspoon salt, ½ teaspoon black pepper, paprika, and nutmeg. Add shrimp to skillet; cook until pink and cooked through, 3 to 4 minutes. Spoon shrimp and 1 tablespoon melted butter over grits. Garnish with green onion and serve immediately.

Country Sausage & Cheddar Quiche

- **1** pound hot country sausage, cooked and drained
- **½** cup sweet onion, diced
- **8** ounces button mushrooms, sliced
- **½** tablespoon butter
- **6** eggs, room temperature
- **1** cup half-and-half (or light cream or whole milk), room temperature
- **¼** teaspoon nutmeg
- **½** teaspoon salt
- **1** (9-inch) deep-dish piecrust, unbaked
- **1** cup shredded Cheddar cheese
- Chives, chopped (optional)

Preheat oven to 400°. Crumble cooked sausage and place on a paper towel.

Sauté onion and mushrooms in butter until onions are translucent and mushrooms are browned. Set aside.

Using an electric mixer with a whisk attachment, combine eggs and half-and-half. Whisk for at least 5 minutes. The mixture will be foamy on top. Add nutmeg and salt.

Place sausage on piecrust and pour egg mixture over it. Sprinkle cheese over egg mixture and carefully place onions and mushrooms for a "layering" effect.

Bake for 15 minutes at 400°, then lower oven to 375° for 30 to 40 minutes, or until center has set. Allow quiche to rest for at least 10 minutes before slicing. Garnish with chopped chives (optional).

HOOP CHEESE BISCUITS

Yield: About 12 biscuits.

- 2 cups biscuit mix
- 1 tablespoon sugar
- ¼ teaspoon black pepper
- ¼ teaspoon cayenne pepper
- ½ teaspoon garlic powder
- ¼ cup chopped chives
- 1 stick cold butter
- 1 cup buttermilk
- 1 pound hoop cheese
- 4 tablespoons butter, melted

Preheat oven to 425°. Grease a muffin tin. In a large bowl, combine biscuit mix, sugar, peppers, garlic powder, and chives. Grate butter into dry ingredients. Using fingers, incorporate to a crumbly consistency. Add buttermilk, a little at a time, until the batter is thick and creamy.

Put 1 heaping tablespoon of mixture in each muffin cup. Pinch off ¾-inch chunks of cheese, and place in the center of the batter. Spoon about 1 heaping tablespoon of batter over each piece of cheese, pushing it around the edges to seal in cheese.

Bake for about 12 minutes, until golden brown. Remove biscuits, and brush them with melted butter. Serve immediately.

— Wendy Perry

Bacon & Egg Cups

Yield: 4 servings.

- 8 slices thick-cut bacon
- 4 large eggs
- 2 sprigs fresh thyme
- 2 tablespoons grated Parmesan cheese
- Salt and black pepper to taste
- 2 green onions, chopped

Preheat oven to 375°. Parcook the bacon slices by frying them for 2 to 3 minutes. Remove bacon from the skillet and drain on paper towels.

Spray a metal muffin pan with cooking spray. Taking one slice of bacon at a time, wrap the inside of a muffin cup to create a ring. Repeat with the remaining slices of bacon (2 slices of bacon per muffin cup).

Carefully crack one egg into each bacon-lined cup. Sprinkle each egg with thyme leaves, Parmesan cheese, salt, and pepper. Bake the egg cups for 10 to 15 minutes, until the centers have set. You can adjust the cooking time based on how you prefer the consistency of your egg yolks.

Carefully remove the bacon-egg cups to a plate. Sprinkle the tops with green onions, and serve immediately with your choice of sides, such as toast, crispy potatoes, grits, or a green salad.

Collard Green & Country Ham Strata

Yield: 6 servings.

2 to 4 teaspoons vegetable oil

1 medium sweet onion, chopped

1 shallot, chopped

½ teaspoon salt

2 pieces thinly sliced country ham, cut into strips

2 cups fresh collard greens, destemmed, washed, and cut into thin ribbons

1 red bell pepper, chopped
6 large eggs
1½ cups whole milk
3 green onions, sliced
Hot sauce (optional)

Preheat oven to 375°. Prepare a round baking dish with oil.

Add vegetable oil to skillet and heat over medium. Add onion and shallot. Sprinkle with ½ teaspoon salt and cook until onion and shallot are translucent, approximately 5 minutes. Remove onion mixture from skillet and set aside.

Return skillet to stove and add country ham. If skillet is dry, add an additional 2 teaspoons of oil. Cook ham until edges begin to brown. Add collard greens to skillet and stir. Add chopped red pepper and continue to cook for 15 minutes, stirring occasionally.

Place collard green and ham mixture in a large mixing bowl. Allow to cool for 10 to 15 minutes.

In a separate bowl, whisk together eggs and milk. Pour half of the egg mixture into the prepared baking dish. Add collard green mixture and top with remaining egg mixture. Sprinkle top with sliced green onions.

Bake, uncovered, for approximately 30 minutes or until the center has set and the top is lightly browned. Remove from oven and let sit for 5 minutes. Serve with hot sauce, if desired.

Sweet Potato Biscuits With Country Ham

Yield: 15 (2½-inch) biscuits.

- 2½ cups all-purpose flour
- 1 tablespoon baking powder
- 1 teaspoon fine sea salt
- ¼ cup packed light brown sugar
- ¾ teaspoon ground cinnamon
- ½ teaspoon ground ginger
- ½ teaspoon ground allspice
- ½ teaspoon ground mace or nutmeg
- ½ cup vegetable shortening
- 1 cup baked sweet potato purée
- 1 cup heavy cream
- Additional all-purpose flour, for rolling
- Country ham, sliced paper-thin

Preheat the oven to 350°. Line a baking sheet with parchment paper or a silicone baking mat.

Mix together the flour, baking powder, salt, brown sugar, cinnamon, ginger, allspice, and mace in a large bowl. Use a pastry blender or your fingertips to work in the shortening until the mixture is crumbly.

Stir together the sweet potato purée and cream in a small bowl. Pour into the flour mixture and stir only until the dough comes together and pulls in all of the dry ingredients.

Pour the dough onto a lightly floured surface and gently knead until smooth and supple, about 8 turns. Roll or pat the dough to a ¾-inch thickness. Stamp out the biscuits with a round cutter. If the dough sticks, dip the cutter into some flour. Push the cutter straight down without twisting so that the biscuits can rise to their full potential. Place the biscuits on the prepared baking sheet. Gather, roll, and cut the dough scraps.

Bake until the biscuits are firm and spring back when lightly touched on top, about 20 minutes. Transfer to a wire rack to cool to room temperature. Store at room temperature in an airtight container overnight before serving. (These biscuits are not great served warm.)

Serve with room-temperature, paper-thin slices of country ham.

— *Sheri Castle*

Breakfast Burritos With Spicy Avocado Salsa

Yield: 4 servings.

FOR THE SALSA:
- 2 ripe avocados, diced
- 1 sweet red bell pepper, diced
- 2 green onions, thinly sliced
- 1 clove garlic, minced
- 1 jalapeño pepper, seeded and minced
- 3 tablespoons fresh lime juice
- ½ teaspoon salt
- ¼ cup fresh chopped cilantro

FOR THE BURRITOS:
- 6 large eggs
- ¼ teaspoon smoked paprika
- ½ teaspoon salt
- 1 pound hot ground breakfast sausage
- 8 ounces shredded Monterey Jack cheese
- 4 (12-inch) flour tortillas
- Vegetable oil

For the salsa: Place all ingredients in a medium bowl and mix to combine. Cover with plastic wrap and refrigerate.

For the burritos: In a medium bowl, whisk eggs with smoked paprika and salt. Set aside.

Cook sausage in a large nonstick pan over medium-high heat. Stir frequently, until browned, 4 to 5 minutes. Use a slotted spoon to transfer sausage from the pan to a plate, leaving the drippings in the pan. Reduce heat to low. Add eggs and soft scramble until eggs are just cooked through. Transfer eggs to a plate.

To assemble: Spoon about ¼ cup of salsa onto the center of each tortilla, followed by a quarter of the sausage, a quarter of the eggs, and 2 ounces or ¼ cup of cheese. Fold in sides of the tortilla over the filling and roll, tucking in the edges as you go.

Lightly coat a nonstick pan with oil and set over medium heat. When the pan is hot, add burritos, seam side down. Cook, covered, until the bottoms of the burritos are golden brown, about 3 minutes. Flip burritos over and continue cooking, covered, until lightly toasted. Serve warm.

There may be extra salsa; use to garnish or enjoy with chips.

Skillet-Fried Sausage & Hominy

Yield: 4 to 6 servings.

- **2** tablespoons unsalted butter, cold
- **1** large sweet onion, chopped
- **2** cloves garlic, crushed
- **¼** teaspoon ground chili powder or chipotle powder
- **Salt to taste**
- **1** pound ground sausage, cooked and drained
- **1** (15½-ounce) can white hominy, drained
- **¼** cup whole milk
- **4** large eggs
- **2** teaspoons fresh cilantro, finely chopped
- **Pepper to taste**
- **Hot sauce (optional)**

In a large sauté pan, melt the butter over medium heat. Add the onions, crushed garlic, chili powder, and salt. Sauté until the onions are soft, about 5 minutes.

Add the sausage and hominy. Stir and cook for another 2 minutes. Stir in the milk and cook until the milk is almost absorbed by the hominy.

Whisk the eggs and add them to the sausage and hominy mixture. Stir and cook on low heat for an additional 3 to 5 minutes. Stir in the cilantro and add additional salt, pepper, and hot sauce if needed.

Stone-Ground Grits With Country Ham

Yield: 6 servings.

- **4 cups water**
- **1 cup whole milk**
- **1 teaspoon kosher salt, plus more to taste**
- **2 cups uncooked stone-ground grits**
- **3 tablespoons unsalted butter**
- **2 to 3 large slices country ham**
- **1 cup hot water**

For the grits: In a large stockpot, combine water, milk, and salt, and bring to a rolling boil on medium-high heat. Gradually whisk in grits; return to a boil. Continue stirring and reduce heat to medium-low. Simmer, stirring occasionally, until creamy and thickened, 25 to 30 minutes.

Remove pot from heat and stir in butter. Salt to taste. Cover and keep warm until ready to serve.

For the ham: Heat a cast-iron skillet on medium-high heat. Once skillet is hot, add ham and cook for 2 to 3 minutes per side. This may need to be done in batches. When ham is slightly browned on each side, remove from skillet and set aside.

Chop cooked ham into small pieces and mix into grits or add as a topping.

Using the same skillet, add 1 cup of hot water to skillet and stir up any ham bits from the pan. Spoon over grits when ready to serve.

Corned Beef Hash With Fried Eggs

Yield: 4 servings.

2 to 3 tablespoons unsalted butter

1 medium yellow onion, diced (about 1 cup)

3 cups cooked corned beef, sliced ½-inch thick and chopped into 1-inch pieces

2 cups Yukon Gold potatoes, boiled and chopped into 1-inch cubes

2 green onions, sliced

Salt and pepper to taste

2 to 4 eggs, fried

Melt butter in a large skillet (preferably cast iron) on medium heat. Add yellow onion and cook for a few minutes, until translucent.

Add corned beef and potatoes to skillet and spread out evenly. Raise heat to medium-high or high and press down on the mixture with a metal spatula. To ensure a crispy crust, do not stir.

After 3 to 4 minutes, check the bottom of the hash. If nicely browned, use the spatula to flip sections over in the pan to brown on the other side. Press down firmly with the spatula. Continue cooking for another 3 to 4 minutes.

Remove from heat. Stir in green onions, and add salt and pepper to taste. Top with fried eggs and serve.

Buttermilk Drop Biscuits

Yield: 12 small or 6 large biscuits.

- **2 cups all-purpose flour**
- **2 teaspoons baking powder**
- **1 teaspoon baking soda**
- **1 teaspoon sugar**
- **1 teaspoon salt**
- **1 cup whole buttermilk, chilled**
- **8 tablespoons unsalted butter, melted and slightly cooled, plus more for brushing**

Preheat oven to 425°. Line a rimmed baking sheet with parchment paper and lightly grease with cooking spray.

In a large bowl, whisk together flour, baking powder, baking soda, sugar, and salt. In a small bowl, stir together chilled buttermilk and melted butter. The mixture will look curdled. Use a rubber spatula to stir the buttermilk mixture into the flour mixture just until the ingredients are incorporated and the mixture slightly pulls away from the edges of the bowl.

Using a greased ¼-cup measure, portion the dough and drop biscuits onto the prepared baking sheet, spacing each about 1½ inches apart.

Bake biscuits until tops are golden brown, 13 to 15 minutes. Remove from oven and brush with additional melted butter. Serve warm.

SWEET POTATO HASH WITH SAUSAGE & EGGS

Yield: 4 servings.

- ½ **pound ground pork sausage**
- 2 **medium sweet potatoes, peeled and cut into ½-inch cubes**
- 1 **medium sweet onion, chopped**
- 1 **red bell pepper, chopped**
- 1 **yellow bell pepper, chopped**
- ½ **teaspoon smoked paprika**
- ½ **teaspoon red pepper flakes**
- 1 **teaspoon salt**
- 4 **large eggs**
- 2 **green onions, sliced (for garnish)**

Preheat oven to 400°.

Heat a large, oven-safe skillet over medium heat and add sausage. Break up sausage in pan and cook until thoroughly browned. Remove sausage from skillet and place on paper towels to drain, reserving 2 tablespoons of sausage drippings in pan. Return skillet to the stove and add the sweet potatoes, onions, and peppers. Cook on medium heat, stirring occasionally, until sweet potatoes are fork-tender. Sprinkle paprika, red pepper flakes, and salt over potato mixture and toss. Add the sausage and stir to combine.

Make 4 indentations, then crack the eggs into each space. Place the skillet in the oven and bake until eggs are cooked to preference (5 minutes for over-easy, 10 minutes for medium, and 15 minutes for firm). Remove skillet from oven and garnish with green onions.

Crispy Home Fries With Sweet & Spicy Ketchup

Yield: 6 servings.

- 2 tablespoons olive oil
- 1 yellow onion, halved and sliced
- 1 teaspoon smoked paprika
- ½ teaspoon garlic powder
- 1 teaspoon seasoned salt
- ½ teaspoon freshly ground black pepper
- 4 medium russet potatoes, peeled and cut into 1-inch cubes

Preheat oven to 425°. Line a large baking sheet with parchment paper and grease with cooking spray.

Coat the bottom of a heavy-duty sauté pan with 2 tablespoons of olive oil on medium-high heat. Add sliced onion. Cook over low heat for 30 minutes, stirring frequently.

In a large mixing bowl, stir together paprika, garlic powder, salt, and pepper. Add potatoes to the seasoning mixture, tossing until evenly coated.

Spread the potatoes on the prepared baking sheet in a single layer and bake until golden brown, about 25 to 30 minutes. In a large bowl, combine home fries with onions and serve.

SWEET & SPICY KETCHUP

Yield: 1 cup.

- 1 cup ketchup
- 1 teaspoon apple cider vinegar
- ½ teaspoon chili powder
- 1 teaspoon sugar
- 1 teaspoon Sriracha or hot sauce
- 1 teaspoon soy sauce

In a small mixing bowl, combine all ingredients. Refrigerate until ready to serve.

Fried Pork Tenderloin Biscuit

Yield: 4 to 6 biscuits.

FOR THE BISCUITS:
- 2 cups self-rising flour
- 1 teaspoon salt
- 1 teaspoon ground black pepper
- 3 tablespoons unsalted butter, very cold, cut into small cubes
- 1¼ cups buttermilk, divided

- 1 teaspoon ground black pepper
- ¼ teaspoon cayenne pepper
- 2 cups cornflakes, crushed
- 2 cups instant flour
- Peanut oil, for frying
- Heirloom tomato, sliced (for serving)
- Texas Pete (for serving)

Preheat oven to 475°. In a large bowl, whisk together flour, salt, and pepper. Using a pastry blender or fork, cut butter into flour until the mixture resembles coarse sand. Make a well in the center of the flour and pour in 1 cup of buttermilk. Turning the edge of the bowl, add flour to buttermilk until all liquid has been absorbed. Do not overmix.

Place dough onto a clean, floured surface and knead 3 or 4 times, folding the dough over each time. Use hands to spread dough out to ½-inch thickness. Using a 3- to 4-inch biscuit cutter, cut out biscuits, dipping the cutter in flour between each biscuit.

Place biscuits on a large baking sheet. Brush the tops with remaining buttermilk. Bake for 12 to 15 minutes or until tops are lightly browned. Remove from oven and tear or slice open.

FOR PORK TENDERLOIN:
- 2 pounds center-cut boneless pork loin
- 2 large eggs
- 2 cups buttermilk
- 1 teaspoon onion powder
- 1 teaspoon kosher salt

Cut the pork crosswise into 4 equal pieces. Without cutting all the way through, slice each piece horizontally until 1 inch of pork remains. Open pork pieces. Place between 2 sheets of plastic wrap. Using a mallet or heavy skillet, pound until ¼-inch thick.

Whisk eggs, buttermilk, onion powder, salt, black pepper, and cayenne in a shallow bowl. Add pork, cover, and refrigerate at least 4 hours or overnight.

Pour crushed cornflakes into a shallow dish. Put flour in another shallow dish. Remove each piece of pork from marinade, letting excess liquid drip off. Dredge both sides in flour, dip into buttermilk marinade again, then coat with crushed cornflakes.

Heat ¼ to ½ inch of peanut oil in a large, heavy-bottom skillet over medium-high heat until a deep-fry thermometer registers 360°. Fry pork in batches until golden and cooked through or until internal temperature reaches 145°, about 3 minutes per side. Drain on paper towels.

Place pork inside biscuits and serve with hot sauce and heirloom tomato slices.

Spring Vegetable Frittata

Yield: 6 servings.

- 2 tablespoons extra-virgin olive oil
- 2 tablespoons unsalted butter
- 1 small sweet onion, diced (about ½ cup)
- 1 pound thin asparagus,
  trimmed and cut into 1-inch pieces
- 1 cup frozen peas
- 1 cup baby spinach
- 3 green onions, sliced
- ¼ teaspoon ground black pepper
- 1 teaspoon smoked paprika
- 8 large eggs
- ½ cup heavy cream
- 1 teaspoon salt
- ½ cup feta cheese, crumbled
- Fresh basil leaves, chopped
  (for garnish)

Preheat oven to 400°.

In a large ovenproof or cast-iron skillet, heat oil and butter over medium heat for 1 minute. Add sweet onion and sauté until translucent, about 3 minutes.

Stir in asparagus and cook until just tender, about 2 minutes. Do not overcook.

Stir in peas, spinach, and green onions. Season with pepper and paprika. Stir vegetables until evenly combined, allowing them to soften.

In a large mixing bowl, whisk together eggs and heavy cream until smooth. Whisk in salt. Pour egg mixture into the skillet and gently stir with a rubber spatula to distribute vegetables. Sprinkle Feta cheese evenly on top.

Bake for 20 minutes, until frittata is completely set or until edges are light golden brown and pulling away from the skillet. Remove from oven and let rest for 5 to 10 minutes.

Garnish with basil and extra feta on top, if desired. Slice and serve.

COFFEE & DOUGHNUTS

Coffee and doughnuts hold the power to bring people together — and North Carolina boasts the best of both. So go ahead. Sip. Dip. Take a bite.

written by KATIE SAINTSING

The doughnuts that roll off conveyor belts today got their start in a brick storefront in what's now Old Salem.

KRISPY KREME

WINSTON-SALEM // The story of doughnuts in North Carolina begins in 1937, when Vernon Rudolph opened up shop with a recipe purchased from a New Orleans chef. The rest came later: the paper hats, the "Hot Now" light, the goodwill for the person who picks up a dozen — of course they'll share — in the iconic white-and-green box. You can imagine the thrill Rudolph must have felt when he took that first bite. You've felt it, too, many times over: the thin layer of sweet glaze giving way to the warm interior, just chewy enough to sink your teeth into. The sensation is unmistakable. And although it's available around the globe now — of course we'll share — we know there's a taste of North Carolina in every bite.

krispykreme.com

Tate Street Coffee

GREENSBORO // "Espresso culture" had not yet arrived in North Carolina when Matt Russ opened a coffee shop on Tate Street, the tight-knit business district that hugs the eastern edge of UNC Greensboro's campus. Russ's new landlord was concerned. "How are you going to make a living selling *coffee*?" he asked. But Russ was inspired by a romantic notion of the Beat Generation and coffeehouses of the 1950s: As a student at UNCG, he'd often hung out in the cafeteria, sipping coffee and doing homework. In 1993, Tate Street Coffee House opened in the space that had been the Friar's Cellar, a gourmet convenience store. "What I liked about Friar's and wanted to bring to Tate Street Coffee was that the students and professors would hang out there, but also artists and lawyers," Russ says. "This is a window between the university and the town."

334 Tate Street, (336) 275-2754

Much of Tate Street's core menu has remained the same since the 1990s, including the best-selling Black & Tan — a latte flavored with chocolate, caramel, and vanilla.

LOCAL LION

Boone

Local Lion is best-known for owners Meredith and Josiah Davis's award-winning potato doughnuts, scratch-made using a 1930s recipe, and their small-batch coffee, which is roasted daily. The Davises — who met as students at Appalachian State University — see the shop as a supportive "base camp" for the community, which inspired its slogan: "Conquer your mountain."

791 Blowing Rock Road, (828) 386-1120

Dripolator

BLACK MOUNTAIN

Try the house-roasted coffee or one of the specialty drinks, like the Golden Milk latte, made with turmeric, ginger, cinnamon, black pepper, and honey.

221 West State Street, (828) 669-0999

BRITT'S DONUT SHOP
Carolina Beach

There is a doughnut on the Carolina Beach Boardwalk that defines the taste of summer. It doesn't have sprinkles or frosting or filling. Doesn't need 'em. The glazed doughnut that Harvey Britt created in 1939 has never gone out of style.

13 Carolina Beach Avenue North
(910) 707-0755

One of the most popular drinks at the cozy café at 21-A North Front Street is the Mochaccino (opposite), a latte made with Ghirardelli chocolate and topped with whipped cream.

PORT CITY JAVA

WILMINGTON // When Port City Java opened in 1995, Steve Schnitzler was the executive chef at Front Street Brewery next door, and he'd stop by for coffee almost daily. He soon joined the company, and now, as CEO, he's helped oversee PCJ's expansion to more than 20 locations in North and South Carolina. Each café has its own personality, but they all have at least one thing in common: Every cup of coffee is made with beans roasted by local folks in Wilmington. And the Front Street shop, now two doors down from the original, remains PCJ's flagship location, embodying the lively, historic spirit of downtown Wilmington. After nearly 30 years in the area, many longtime customers say they grew up with the café.
portcityjava.com

At Hole, you'll always find vanilla glazed, toasted-almond sesame cinnamon, and cinnamon sugar, plus a weekly seasonal flavor.

Hole Doughnuts

ASHEVILLE // The month Hole opened in 2014, Hallee Hirsh and Ryan Martin discovered Asheville and fell in love with the city. They were visiting from Los Angeles, searching for a place to raise their growing family closer to the earth. Meanwhile, at Hole, founder Caroline Whatley kept things simple, offering only four doughnut flavors a day and forming the dough by hand so that each was charmingly different. Her bourbon-molasses glazed doughnut soon earned national attention — but by then, Whatley was ready for a new adventure. Hirsh and Martin were delighted to pick up where she left off, keeping the community in coffee and doughnuts: a perfect circle.

168 Haywood Road, (828) 774-5667

TO ORDER MORE

If you've enjoyed *Rise & Shine*, think of your family members, friends, and coworkers who would enjoy it, too! Call the Our State Store at (800) 948-1409, or visit ourstatestore.com.